Sandy Jay

this book will help

you enjoy the things your

father so enjoyed in the

grand "out-doors"

Love from

Aunt Nancy * Uncle Stums

The Golden Book of
NATURE CRAFTS

HOBBIES AND ACTIVITIES FOR BOYS AND GIRLS

by JOHN R. SAUNDERS
Chairman, Department of Public Instruction
The American Museum of Natural History

Photographs by ROY PINNEY

Drawings by RENE MARTIN
and by JAMES GORDON IRVING, DOROTHEA AND SY BARLOWE, RAYMOND PERLMAN, AND ARNOLD W. RYAN

GOLDEN PRESS · NEW YORK

The author and publisher wish to acknowledge with thanks the cooperation of WOMAN'S DAY magazine in preparing this book. All of the articles and most of the photographs first appeared in the pages of WOMAN'S DAY, and are reprinted here by permission.

Grateful acknowledgment is made to James Gordon Irving, whose drawings on pages 50-51 first appeared in the Golden Nature Guide STARS; his drawings on page 11, and the Baltimore oriole on page 33, first appeared in the Golden Nature Guide BIRDS; the mouse, rabbit, fox, muskrat, mole and prairie dog, on pages 32-33, first appeared in the Golden Nature Guide MAMMALS; the drawings on pages 63, 64, 67 and the mud dauber and paper wasps on pages 32-33, first appeared in the Golden Nature Guide INSECTS. Acknowledgment is also made to Dorothea and Sy Barlowe, whose drawings on pages 56-57 are from the Golden Nature Guide TREES, and whose drawing of a hermit crab, on page 33, is from the Golden Nature Guide SEASHORES; to Raymond Perlman, whose drawings on pages 17 and 19 are from the Golden Nature Guide ROCKS AND MINERALS; and to Arnold W. Ryan, whose drawings on pages 26-27 first appeared in the Basic Science Education Series, "Toads and Frogs," © copyright 1942, Row, Peterson and Company.

CONTENTS

ABOUT THIS BOOK

THE GOLDEN BOOK OF NATURE CRAFTS is full of suggestions for things that young people can *do* with nature. It introduces nature study by offering many exciting ways to explore our natural surroundings. It tells of things to collect and of things to make; of things to grow and of things to watch: collecting birds' feathers, making leaf prints, growing sweet potato vines, observing fireflies—these are but a few of the suggested projects.

The activities selected for this book require only a few simple tools and inexpensive pieces of equipment. Some of the equipment can actually be made rather than bought. The step-by-step directions for each activity are briefly and clearly stated. If they are followed carefully, they will lead to satisfying experiences.

We are grateful to the publishers of *Woman's Day* magazine for permission to use this material, all of which originally appeared as a series of articles in their magazine. It is our hope that the young people who use NATURE CRAFTS will get as much pleasure from their experiences as did the author and his children when they tested each of these activities.

JOHN R. SAUNDERS

Chairman, Department of Public Instruction

The American Museum of Natural History

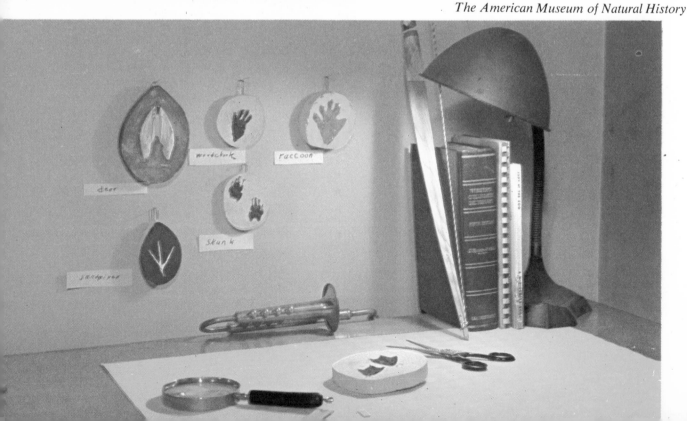

Mount feathers on sheets of construction paper with strips of transparent gummed tape.

Feathers Are Fabulous

You can turn a hike or stroll through the woods into a treasure hunt by keeping eyes open for feathers that birds shed. Birds lose feathers when they molt, fly through thickets, or have a close brush with the enemy.

The nice thing about collecting their cast-off plumage is that you don't have to set out especially for that purpose. Feathers of every form, size, shape, and color lie in all kinds of places to catch your eye when you camp, picnic, or take a stroll. Even while out on an errand, you might pick up a breath-taking beauty, shed by a robin redbreast or a ruby-throated hummingbird.

To be a collector, you'll need paper envelopes for storing feathers and a guidebook by which to identify your discoveries. As your collection grows, knowledge of these winged gypsies and their amazing flying gear will grow along with it. Later, you may want to move feathers from paper envelopes into show-off plastic envelopes, mount your specimens on stiff paper, or keep them in a box or tray.

Where to Look: Feathers can be found almost anywhere at any time. Late summer and early fall are when most birds molt, but quite often feathers are to be found where birds feed or nest. (Don't disturb the nest.) You may find feathers shaken loose around shallow pools where birds go bathing or in dusting spots along the roads, where they thrash about in dust baths. If you accidentally flush (or frighten) a bird into flight, look about to see if a few feathers haven't fallen.

What Is a Feather?: It's an epidermal growth allied to the scale of a reptile but not to the hair of a mammal. Although there are interesting variations or modifications, there are basically three major types:

Down feathers: Small, very soft, they are not so strong-stemmed as flight feathers. They are to protect the bird against both cold weather and the burning sun.

Contour feathers: Firm but often downy at the base, they form the main body covering.

Flight feathers: The larger, stronger-stemmed feathers of wings and tail. When molting, most birds do not shed all flight feathers at once; thus, they're never without flight equipment. However, ducks, rails, loons, and other water birds are unable to fly during the molting period because they drop *all* their flight feathers.

In the typical flight feather, you'll find a strong tapering central stem or shaft. The lower, thicker end is called the "quill"; it is hollow. The upper section is called the

Protect feathers by bringing them home in envelopes.

A magnifying glass reveals details of construction.

"rachis"; it's filled with a firm pith. The entire shaft will stand a lot of bending before breaking. Radiating outward on each side of the shaft are hundreds of thin structures called "barbs"; they form the feather's body or vane.

To see the real marvel, use a microscope or hand lens to study a feather. Look for the tiny hairlike branches called "barbules" that range along each side of each barb. Those on the side nearest the base of the feather are curved and notched at the end; they are called "ciliae." Those on the side toward the outer tip of the feather end are hooked; they are called "hamuli."

When a feather is in proper shape, each barb is hooked to its adjoining barb. This marvelous design of interlocking hooks and notches enables the feather to hold air. Otherwise, the bird would not be able to fly, because pressure on the feather in attempted flight would cause the barbs to separate and the air to slip through.

LOCATION OF FEATHERS

How to Arrange Your Collection: Take your pick of any of the following ways. One way is to keep a sheet of paper for each species and, on this sheet, mount and label a down feather, a contour feather, a wing and tail (or flight) feather. Or you might like to make a comparison collection and mount on each sheet different examples of certain types of feathers, such as a down feather from each of ten different kinds of birds. Another way is to arrange your collection according to color or according to the markings of the feathers.

How to Identify Feathers: Use a guidebook. Study the illustrations and descriptions in your guidebook to learn what bird your feather came from. If there's a natural history museum near you, compare its bird collections with your feather specimens.

A FEATHER SEEN THROUGH A MAGNIFYING GLASS

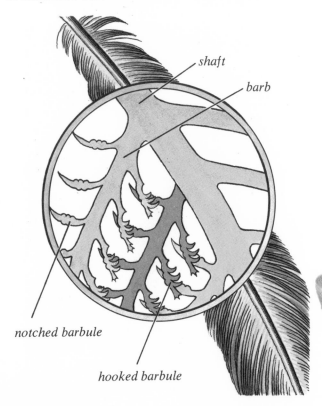

shaft

barb

notched barbule

hooked barbule

TYPES OF BODY FEATHERS

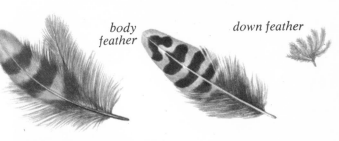

body feather

down feather

body feather with aftershaft

11

Casting Animal Tracks

If you are curious, like to create things, and are a collector at heart, then casting animal tracks is for you.

A plaster cast is easy to make. All the materials you need are: a package of plaster of Paris or dental plaster; a bowl; a spoon or stick; cardboard; a paper clip; a small bottle of tempera paint; and a paintbrush.

Actual tracks rarely have perfect detail. Better tracks for casting can be found in spring, summer, and fall than in winter. However, tracks can be found all year round in the South and along sandy beaches. Easiest to cast are those in mud or clay; most difficult, in snow and dry sand. Best places to look are on trails along stream banks, and in the woods after a rain.

Step 1 *After finding track, carefully brush away twigs, small stones, and excess dirt found in its immediate vicinity.*

The animal-track casts you make can be turned into interesting wall decorations.

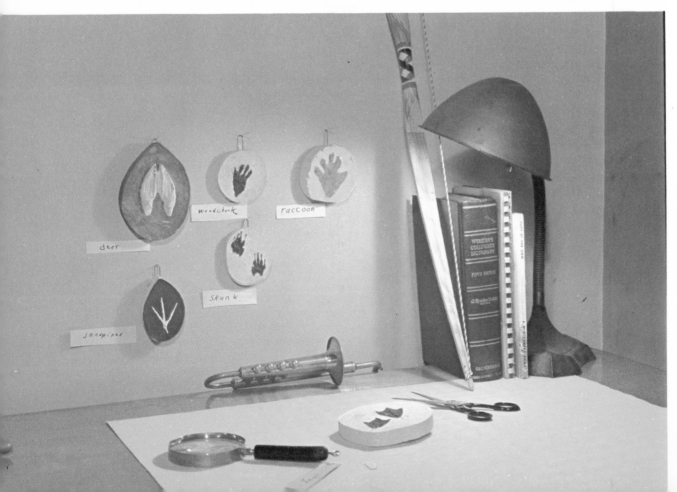

Step 2 *Use cardboard strip 1½ inches wide to surround track. Fasten strip with paper clip to form a dam. Push down lightly into dirt.*

Step 3 *Mix plaster of Paris to consistency of thick cream (put plaster into water—not water into plaster!). Pour slowly over track.*

Step 4 *After plaster hardens, about 30 minutes, lift out, peel cardboard away. Painting is finishing touch.*

SOME EASY ANIMAL TRACKS TO FIND

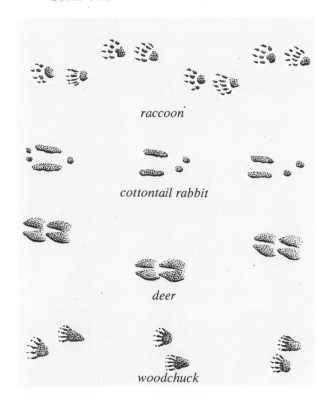

raccoon

cottontail rabbit

deer

woodchuck

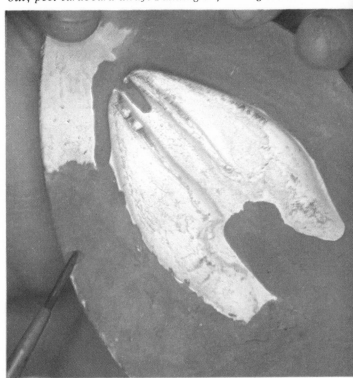

Sammy Skunk Snaps His Own Picture

When you catch night-prowling animals with your "camera trap" you have a hobby which actually combines two. One is photography, from which you'll learn quite a lot of camera craft. The other is nature study, which will introduce you to creatures you rarely meet and will reveal habits that differ from those of day-time animals.

You'll need a loaded camera with shutter-release lever and attached synchronized flash gun. Also have a spool of strong black thread, snap mousetrap, wooden peg, adhesive tape, screw eye, and some bait, such as leftover beef bone. Shield camera from rain with clear plastic refrigerator bag.

Tape camera and flash attachment to tree,

Put up a sign so that others won't disturb your "camera trap."

using a wedge between tree and camera to angle it downward. Tape mousetrap below camera to tree, angling spring bar downward. Push peg in ground near tree, twist in screw eye, run thread through. Tie end of thread firmly to bait, placing bait within camera focus. Run thread from peg to mousetrap. Cut from spool, tie tautly to bait hook. Cut off another piece of thread and tie it loosely from mousetrap's spring to camera's shutter-release lever. Being careful of fingers, set mousetrap and test camera by pulling at bait until you're sure arrangement works. Roll fresh film into position, put in flash bulb, carefully set mousetrap again. Now, cover with plastic bag with hole cut in front of camera lens, making sure bag doesn't interfere with shutter release. Leave trap overnight and see what happens.

What Kind of Camera? Any kind of camera from a simple box type up to the finest can be used, just so long as it has flash equipment

This picture was taken by Sammy Skunk himself!

that works. But using a fine camera is not advised. The less expensive, the better, because you'll be leaving this equipment out of doors, and you don't want to tempt someone to walk off with it.

Where to Set Up "Camera Trap"? Animals' footprints are sometimes a clue as to where to set up the trap. Raccoons and mink, for example, prowl around stream beds; deer and bear along the edge of open fields; opossum in wooded sections; the skunk wherever he can find anything to eat.

What Kind of Bait? When you put out the food animals love to eat, your bait problem is solved. If you're aiming at a deer, for instance, a small piece of salt block would be an irresistible lure. To make, put some table salt, about ½ pound, in a paper box, dampen and let it dry into a hard cake.

Skunks and other omnivorous animals will eat both vegetables and meat. The raccoon, opossum, and skunk go for corn on the cob, beef bones, and other leftovers. The opossum and raccoon like fruit, too, especially peaches.

HOW TO SET UP A "CAMERA TRAP"

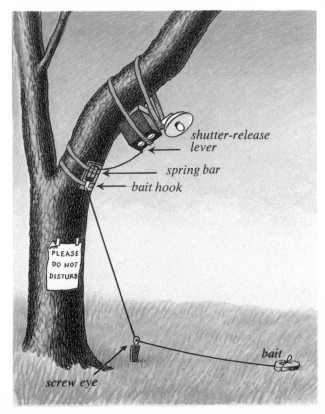

shutter-release lever

spring bar

bait hook

PLEASE DO NOT DISTURB

bait

screw eye

15

How To Be A Rock Hound

A treasure hunt for rocks and minerals can be as exciting as digging for a pirate's buried chest. The rarer the specimens and the more beautiful the colors and forms, the more rewarding you'll find the quest.

This hobby could lead to a vocation in the geological, chemical, or engineering sciences. Right now, it offers the fun and interest of finding specimens other collectors will admire, and trading with other rock hounds to improve your collection.

There is usually good hunting for a beginning rock hound right around you. Later, you can go farther afield for even richer finds which, besides minerals and rocks, will be scenic beauties and interesting folklore.

Type of Equipment: Prying small chunks from cliffsides, or working delicate minerals out of bedrock, calls for the use of tools and some skill. Hand in hand with a strong hammer, use a cold chisel (all-metal, for chipping stone) from ¼- to 1-inch wide. These can be bought at hardware and some dime stores. You'll need a pocket magnifier or small hand lens for examining specimens, bought at stationery and some cutlery shops and through some mail-order catalogs.

A collecting sack can be made at home of any sturdy fabric. Used Army-and-Navy store Musette or gas-mask bags are also good.

It's a good idea to have a supply of newspaper for wrapping up specimens and a small

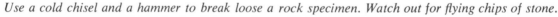

Use a cold chisel and a hammer to break loose a rock specimen. Watch out for flying chips of stone.

pad and pencil with which to record data in the field. After specimen is pried loose, write name, if you can identify it, on a piece of paper, along with the date and locality. Then wrap this with the specimen in newspaper and tuck into your collecting sack.

Size of Specimens: Try to keep stones you pry out about the size of a walnut. If it's a piece of crystal or a type of rock occurring in a narrow vein, it will very often be smaller. And you'll find that some pebbles and rock fragments will be so small you won't have to use any tools on them.

Where to Go: The best sources are excavations in bedrock for the foundations of new buildings; road-cuts through solid rocks; mine dump heaps; quarries; mountains and hills with exposed bedrock; boulders left behind by

FIELD EQUIPMENT NEEDED FOR ROCK HOUNDING

PROTECT SPECIMENS WITH NEWSPAPER WRAPPING

Before wrapping specimen in newspaper, record name (if known) and locality where it was found.

A pocket magnifying glass is a valuable aid in identifying specimens in the field.

How To Be A Rock Hound *(continued)*

glaciers, which are scattered throughout our northern regions.

Always obtain permission to collect on private property, including mines or quarries. Never collect in national, state, or city parks. Always be careful when you climb mountains, and remember to watch out for snakes.

What to Collect: For the most fun, collect with a purpose: for color and texture, on a geographical basis, or for something specialized, such as ores or semi-precious stones.

Whatever the purpose, keep a record, and make sure your identification is correct. Good

handbooks will help you to identify your finds. Also, comparison of these with museum collections, will be useful.

Care of Collection: As the number of specimens increases, you will want a place to keep them. Safekeeping is necessary, as some minerals are softer than others and cannot be jumbled together without being scratched or marred.

So, early in this game, get a compartmented box or tray. There are various kinds. One might be the drawers of an old chest, which you can partition with masonite, beaverboard, or plain cardboard. Spaces should be about 2

18

A good guidebook will help verify identification when you get the specimen home.

inches by 3 inches and about 3 inches high.

Another kind might be a cabinet bought from a junk or secondhand shop or inexpensive plastic compartmented trays or boxes. If you're handy with tools, make the tray exactly as you want it.

Keep Rocks in Order: Since you'll want to refer to your collection as new specimens are added, and show it to others (part of the fun), you'll want to keep your rocks in neat order. Paste a number, typed or printed in ink, on each rock. Or print consecutive numbers on a strip of adhesive tape; cut off, one at a time, to stick on each specimen.

In each compartment, along with the numbered specimen, put a neatly lettered or typed label on a small white card, about 1½ inches by 2½ inches. This will give you enough space to put on it specimen number, date, and locality.

Label specimen and write data on card before adding new rocks to your collection.

Spider Webs Are Amazing

To watch a spider at work is worth all the time you can spend observing his geometrically precise turns and spins. As a spinner, he can't be beat. As an engineer, his feats rank with man's sky-reaching towers, man's river-spanning bridges.

Collecting spiders' webs—when their builders aren't around or after you've urged them off the premises—takes only a little skill and equipment. As your hand becomes steadier and your search yields better specimens, you'll experience the thrill of having captured for keeps the elusive magic of a spider's web.

The flat wheel-shape web of the orb-web spider is ideal for mounting. Less desirable to collect are the shapeless masses, three-dimensional patterns, and funnel-shape webs.

Equipment: The beginner may need turpentine; a piece of old cloth for removing paint; newspapers to keep paint off shrubbery.

Other equipment needed is white enamel, in a spray-top can (colored enamels can be used, but white is best against dark paper);

construction paper (which comes in packets of 50 sheets, 9 inches by 12 inches); an old pair of scissors.

Where to Search: During the summer and fall, wheel-shape webs may be found on branches of small trees, shrubs, or fence rails. The web is a trap to catch insects. Spiders spin their webs across open spaces to supports that hold the long threads that act as guy lines.

How to Collect: After locating web, put newspapers in place, as a house painter does a drop cloth. Lay out equipment.

If there's a spider on the web, you won't want to kill him. Spiders often feed on injurious insects and so are beneficial.

But don't risk getting bitten by trying to pick one up or even touching it. Only a few have dangerous bites, but those of others can be annoying. To speed a spider off his web, try tickling him with a long twig; usually, he'll exit along a guy line to nearby cover.

If a twig or leaf is in your way when you're

Spray paint carefully from a side angle.

After lifting paper up to web, snip guy lines.

ready to ease sheet of construction paper under web, remove without disturbing web or guy lines holding it.

Spray web sparingly from a side angle. Coat both sides, using short bursts of spray to prevent tearing. If there is a breeze, spray with, *not* against it. Don't set out on a windy day, and even on days when there is no high wind, there may be a small breeze to watch out for. Don't stand so that you'll breathe in any paint.

When all threads of the web have been lightly coated, ease paper close to underside or back of web, depending on its position. Now, carefully try to touch paper to the whole web at once, keeping hand steady.

To pull or twist paper now will spoil the web. Making sure sticky web and paper are one, snip off guy lines at paper's edges, and set it aside to dry.

How to Keep Your Collection: Put mounted webs in a scrapbook or frame and hang as wall decorations. They can also be placed under glass on a serving tray or coffee table.

HOW
A SPIDER
CONSTRUCTS
HIS WEB

Step 1 *Spider begins web by dropping thread from A on top branch to A¹ on bottom branch. He climbs up thread A¹ to A, along branch to B, drops thread from B to B¹; then he climbs up thread B¹ to C and starts new thread at C. Trailing thread, he climbs from C to B to A, and fixes thread to C¹ after drawing it tight.*

Step 2 *Spider climbs from C¹ to A, to D drops to thread C¹-C at point D¹, attaches thread, climbs back thread to D and pulls it tight.*

Step 3 *He constructs radial threads E to E¹, A¹ to F, G to G¹, etc., until he reaches I.*

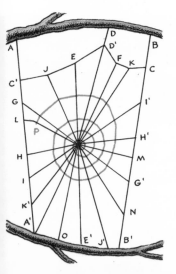

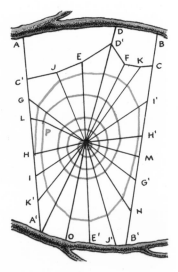

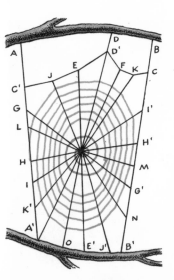

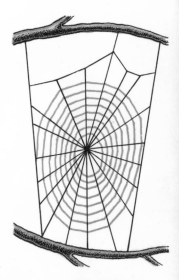

Step 4 *He adds radial threads J to O, then begins adding primary spiral (shown in red), starting at center and ending at P.*

Step 5 *Spider now starts adding sticky threads (shown in blue), working from outside to center.*

Step 6 *Spider continues adding spirals of sticky thread, meanwhile cutting away the original threading of the primary, or scaffold, spiral.*

Step 7 *Web is finished. All primary spiral thread is removed; only sticky thread and supporting threads remain.*

Window Gardens From Kitchen Cuttings

One of your triumphs as a window gardener will be in seeing fugitives from the garbage pail become flourishing house plants. You'll enjoy turning kitchen cuttings—beet, radish, carrot, parsnip, and pineapple tops—and citrus fruit and avocado seeds into a Cinderella garden. You may even want to take some whole specimens and grow trailing vines from a sweet potato, or lacy sprays of greenery from half a carrot which, turned upside down, you can hang up like a little basket.

Such plants will grow in almost any kind of container. Some will flourish in water. Others will need potting soil which your garden will probably yield or you can buy from the neighborhood florist or five-and-dime store. Where pebbles and gravel are needed for anchoring plants in shallow bowls, you can find these in your driveway, along the roadside, or at the seashore.

Carrot, Beet, Radish, and Parsnip Cuttings: These mean the tops of such vegetables which, trimmed off, usually land in the garbage pail. If as much as the top inch or so is saved, they will make attractive foliage. Trim the green leaves to within ¼ inch of the top. Place, with their stems up, in a shallow dish of water; and anchor, to hold them upright, with some clean pebbles or gravel. A dozen or more cuttings from carrots, for example, will sprout lush foliage and will produce a lacy white flower.

Avocado Seed: The big seed removed from the avocado (or alligator pear), before serving, will grow into a tall umbrella-like plant. Place the seed in a glass or jar of water, with the pointed end up, so that one third of it is kept wet. If the seed is small, you can suspend it from the rim of the glass by sticking toothpicks into the side. Keep in a fairly dark place. Look for the white root to appear in about 3 weeks.

When the plant is 6 or 7 weeks old, it's time to think of putting it into a pot. So, gradually add sand to the water, as this will protect the roots when you plant the sprouted seed. Use a pot about 5½ inches high, filled with sandy soil to within ½ inch of the top to allow for watering.

Pineapple Tops: If the top inch of a pineapple is cut off, it will grow into an interesting plant. To get one of these going, you'll need a pot of sandy soil, large enough to give the plant

Sweet potatoes will grow into flourishing vines.

Use an apple corer to hollow out top of carrot.

roomy quarters in which to expand. When roots have formed, which will take about 3 or 4 weeks, transplant into a pot nearly full of rich soil. Give this tropical beauty warmth and plenty of water.

Sweet-Potato or Yam Vine: One that already has a few whiskers is the best choice. Set it, with the end with the most whiskers (usually the narrow end) down, in a tumbler, jar, or bowl of water with one third of the potato submerged. If necessary to hold it up, push toothpicks into the sides of the potato and suspend from rim of container. Put in warm, dark place. Add water as needed. Roots will grow first.

In about 10 days, green stems will appear, at which time you can tie a string or hook a wire around the container and hang in a window, preferably in late-afternoon sunshine, which won't wither the plant.

Upside-down Carrot: You'll need an apple corer or paring knife, a nail, some string, and a whole carrot, the larger the better. Since it must have a growing tip, the kind that comes with the green tops trimmed off and packed in cellophane bags won't do because it won't grow feathery fronds.

Cut the top greens off to within ¼ inch of the top of the carrot. Now cut the bottom of the carrot off about 2½ inches from the top end. Scoop out the center of the thick upper section, leaving a shell about ¼ inch thick. Take care not to pierce the shell as the hollowed-out center must be kept filled with water. Before filling, make three holes with the nail, around the top, and through these tiny openings, thread string or ribbon for hanging. It hangs upside-down so that the leafy sprays will grow upward around the carrot—an interesting characteristic of this plant.

Seeds of Citrus Fruit: Save seeds from grapefruits, oranges, and lemons and put in a warm place to dry. Plant several in a shallow pot of garden soil. Don't water too much. Once every two or three days is often enough. In the spring, the seedlings that have been growing steadily since fall can be transplanted into larger pots and placed outdoors where, with just a little bit of encouragement, they will continue to grow. Of course, when cold weather comes, bring them indoors.

Firefly, What Makes You Glow?

A June evening without the twinkling lights of fireflies would be like a June day without roses. There are about 50 different kinds of fireflies in the United States with different colored lights, and different rhythms of flashing their lights. Children love to catch these living flashlights. Put enough of them into a glass jar, and you have a living lamp, aglow with the flashing lights of imprisoned insects.

Two mysteries still surround the firefly. One is: What is the true nature of its "cold" light? It produces no measurable heat. We'd give a lot to be able to produce light without heat.

This much scientists know. The "fuel" in the firefly's light is a substance called *luciferin*. It reacts when it comes in contact with oxygen,

but only when there is present still another substance, called *luciferase*. Also produced by the firefly, *luciferase* acts as a catalyst or "trigger" which enables *luciferin* to consume oxygen and thus give off light. The supply of luciferin does not diminish as it is "burned," another phenomenon that keenly interests us.

The second mystery is: Why the light? Is it a signal flashed by both sexes, which draws the fireflies together for mating? Is the light, warning of an unpleasant taste, a device to keep other creatures from feeding on the fireflies? Or does the light serve as a bait to lure unwary males of one species into the waiting jaws of the hungry females of another? The answer might be "yes" to any one of these.

Exploring A Stream

Whirligig beetles swimming madly about on the surface . . . salamanders gliding along the murky bottom . . . turtles plopping from banks with a noisy splash. . . . That's life in a fresh-water stream, but that's only a sampling of a vast population. Even more creatures come to the stream to feed and drink. Every turn of a stream reveals new forms of life, grass banks to search, rocks to lift.

Even if you don't collect, it's fun to get a closer look at some of the stream's varied citizens. Dipping them up with net or sieve, you can put them in a pan of water, take a leisurely look, then carefully slide them back into the water.

If you're interested in collecting, however, as well as exploring, you might want to start with a polliwog. You'll need, besides the net or sieve, a glass jar in which to take home the polliwog, and a fish bowl to keep him in so that you can observe his astonishing transformation into a frog.

What to Wear: Unless the weather is warm enough to go in barelegged, a pair of wading boots is a must. Even in the summer, it's wise to wear old sneakers to protect feet from rocks and slippery moss.

Where to Go: If you don't intend to collect—only wade and explore—our state and national parks are full of wonderful streams. Before collecting, it is always wise to find out what the rules and regulations are in the particular area. As you know, one cannot collect anything in a state or national park. But, fortunately, our country is blessed with streams and brooks where you *can* collect, most of them small and shallow enough to be quite safe.

Your Gear: It's good to have two kinds of nets: one, a small cloth net with a wire handle, useful for cupping your catch in your hands; the other, a larger type, of wire, such as a kitchen sieve, or large dip net you can make.

One way to make a dip net is with a peach-basket hoop and a piece of plastic screen, cut circular so that it is 2 inches larger in diameter than the hoop. Sew screen to hoop with strong, preferably waxed, thread.

For another kind of dip net you can make —one with which you can cut a wide swath in a stream—you'll need 2 sticks (½ inch dowels are excellent) 2 feet long and a piece of plastic screen about 1 foot by 1½ feet. These dimensions will allow for about 6 inches of stick to extend beyond the screen, to provide handles. To make, simply roll screen over each stick, and tack in place.

You can equip a regular fine-mesh kitchen sieve with a longer handle by attaching a

Homemade dip nets are fine for scooping up a variety of animal life from shallow streams.

Some useful equipment for stream exploration.

This pollywog has just started to grow legs.

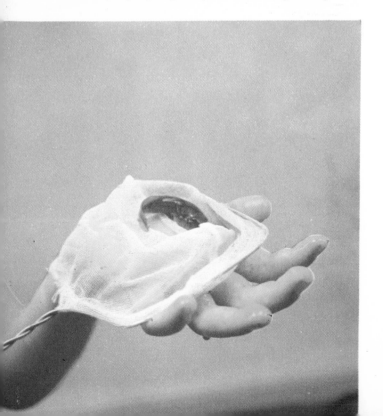

Exploring A Stream (*continued*)

length of ½ inch dowel to the sieve handle.

You'll also need a water-filled glass jar, one with a screw top, for the polliwog you hope to catch. Punch holes in the top so that air can get in.

Glass House for Your Pet: A gallon-size fish bowl, bought at a dime store or pet shop, is just right. Fill the bowl with water to house the tadpole.

When he develops into a frog, use only 2 inches of water, and put in some rocks upon which he can sit. No longer fitted with gills, he'll need to climb above the water. You'll have to put a top on your fish bowl to keep him from hopping out. A top of cotton gauze, held in place with a rubber band, will do. So will a piece of window glass, larger than the bowl, if it's weighted down. If glass is used, insert a small cork or wad of cardboard between top and bowl for air.

LIFE CYCLE OF A FROG

1 *frog eggs*

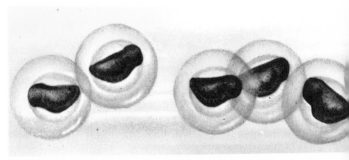

2 *closeup of eggs beginning to develop*

Food for Your Pet: Luckily, a tadpole comes with all the food he needs, stored up in his tail. However, when he matures—begins to grow legs—you'll need to add algae. That's small plant life of a greenish color and a scumlike consistency, which you can find around the edge of ponds and in the water itself. Feed your pet "green water," containing algae and any other growing water-plant material you find in the pond or stream.

When your pet is more than a polliwog—legs almost completely developed, tail practically gone—feed him earthworms, soft insects, flies, grasshoppers, and crickets, which, during mild weather, you can catch in the nearby woods or park.

Later on, he'll be content with meal worms, which you can buy from a pet shop and continue to cultivate yourself. In a can with holes punched in the lid, put meal worms; add some dry oatmeal for food and a few pieces of raw apple for moisture; then set the can aside in

Tempt your pet to eat by dangling food in front of him with a pair of tweezers.

a dark place. Tweezers will be better to use than fingers for picking up meal worms and feeding them to your pet. Dangle them in front of him, and he will snap them up!

3 *newly hatched tadpole*

5 *tadpole with four legs*

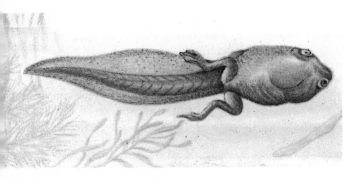

4 *tadpole with hind legs*

6 *frog, tail disappearing*

sugar maple

tuliptree

pin oak

shagbark hickory

Making Leaf Prints

Leaf printing introduces you to the study of plants, another interesting chapter in nature's book. Collecting leaves for printing, and tracking down facts about the trees, bring a richer enjoyment of these forest friends.

The simplest way to make a leaf print is to spatter with ink, using, besides ink, an old toothbrush, colored craft paper, pins, and a stick. Since no other materials are needed except a leaf-drying press, made of old newspapers, this is one of the least expensive of the nature hobbies. It doubles as an art project. Finished leaf prints make keepsake scrapbooks or handsome wall decorations.

For printing, use typical leaves, a help in identifying the tree when you see it again. Search for shapes as nearly perfect as possible and without defects, such as insect holes. The more lobes, or divisions, the leaf has, the more attractive the print will be.

Leaves can be collected along streets, in woodlands, or parks. It's not necessary to pull off leaves. Fallen ones will do as well. Pulling off a single leaf, however, won't deface or damage a tree.

Starting with native trees, you can go on from these to the many cultivated species found on lawns and in gardens.

sassafras

rose

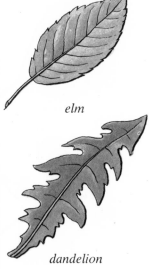

elm

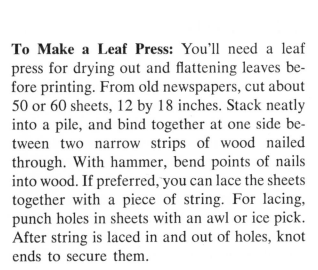

dandelion

Make a leaf press by binding old sheets of newspaper into a book.

When leaf has been pressed long enough so that it lies flat, pin it to sheet of construction paper.

To spatter, dip toothbrush in ink, hold it steady while scraping stick toward, not away, from yourself.

To Make a Leaf Press: You'll need a leaf press for drying out and flattening leaves before printing. From old newspapers, cut about 50 or 60 sheets, 12 by 18 inches. Stack neatly into a pile, and bind together at one side between two narrow strips of wood nailed through. With hammer, bend points of nails into wood. If preferred, you can lace the sheets together with a piece of string. For lacing, punch holes in sheets with an awl or ice pick. After string is laced in and out of holes, knot ends to secure them.

To Spatter Around Leaf: After spreading a large piece of paper over table or other working area to protect it, pour the colored ink into a small dish. Use a stick about 6 inches long to scrape ink from the toothbrush. Scrape the stick through the brush toward you, not away from you. This makes the bristles of the brush snap back away from you to spatter the ink outward, not inward. A little practice first, using water, helps get the hang of spattering before ink is used. Experimenting with ink teaches how to make a fine spatter. When it's fine, the leaf print is more effective than when ink is released in blobs.

Spatter-printing can be used for other designs. Abstracts or other cutouts of blotting paper or various kinds of stencils can be spatter-printed just as effectively as leaves. Fronds of fern also make beautiful designs.

Learn Where Animals Live

The woods are full of animals whose home-building skills could put to shame many a do-it-yourselfer armed with the latest power tools. You'll find among the *master masons* of the animal world, for instance, the mud dauber wasp and the trap-door spider, which make the building materials for the marvelous homes they build; *weavers,* like the Baltimore orioles, whose homes are beautiful "hand-woven" hanging baskets (original rock-a-by babies). For examples of *spinners,* there are the spiders whose homes are the fine silken webs they spin. Among the *papermakers* are the white-faced hornets, which build homes of

Many animals' homes, like this paper-wasp's nest, can be photographed for your collection.

pulp they chew from wood. Beavers are both *lumbermen* and *engineers*—they fell trees and use the cut branches to build dams or lodges.

Animal homes—whether in use or being built—are fun for a young nature lover to discover and add to his knowledge. All the equipment you'll need is sharp eyes, pencil, notebook, sketch pad. Field glasses, too, will help. If you own a camera, use it to catch a picture of an interesting home. While exploring, don't disturb animals.

Here are some categories of homeowners and clues to finding their unlisted addresses:

Above-ground Dwellers: Some build under eaves of houses and barns, others in trees, on small plants, shrubs, grass. A dead tree is a wonderful place to look. If it's standing and hollow, you may find a raccoon, opossum, owl, or woodpecker. Insects and other small creatures may be found living in or under the bark. If a dead tree is lying on the ground, it's apt to house small snakes, slugs, and spiders.

Among tree dwellers are squirrels, good tree pruners, and those skilled papermakers, the white-faced hornets. The hornets chew small pieces of wood until pulpy, mix with gluelike saliva, eject the pulp, and pat it into place in thin sheets with their jaws and feet.

Underground Dwellers: Many dig, tunnel, or burrow underground. The earthworm and mole, for example, stay mostly underground. Wasps use old field mice burrows to build paper nests underground, but fly out to forage for food and water.

Other underground home builders, all efficient diggers, include the woodchuck, fox, chipmunk, badger, prairie dog, many insects, and some spiders.

The trap-door spider and the ant lion use marvelous skill in making traps for prey.

The home of the trap-door spider is a marvel of construction.

The trap-door spider tunnels six or more inches deep, lines the underground tunnel with earth, mixed with a gluelike substance from his mouth. For his house, he makes a snug lid or trap door by spinning a thick, round web the size of the opening. This he covers with a layer of dirt, and spins another round web on top of it. Repeating the operation until the door is as thick as he wants it, he spins a web for hinging it to the tunnel. For camouflage, he sometimes uses bits of moss to thatch his door under which he waits, holding the door ajar with his abdomen, until unsuspecting prey comes along. When the hapless victim does, this Bluebeard seizes it, pops down into the tunnel, and closes the trap door behind him.

The ant lion, another wily one, makes a funnel-shaped pit, and cunningly buries himself almost out of sight at the bottom of it. When an unwary insect falls in, it slides down the sandy sides right into the ant lion's waiting jaws.

Cave Dwellers: Found living in ready-made homes—caves and cavelike niches in rock piles and other formations—are bats, woodrats, and some toads, insects, and salamanders.

Floating Population: Many birds use nests only long enough to lay eggs, set on them, and nurture fledglings until strong enough to fly.

Eccentric Home Dwellers: Among the gangster type that takes over someone else's home is the hermit crab. He pulls the marine snail out of its shell, backs into it, hooks his tail into the lining, and sets off, dragging with him the ready-made home he has stolen.

The house of the log cabin caddis fly is rather odd, too. It's a case built of plant material by the larva of the caddis fly, which lives in water. It looks like a tiny log cabin.

Where to Look for Animals' Homes: Canvass your own back yard, then the neighborhood, nearby parks, woods, and empty fields. Start a

31

NATURE'S CREATURES USE A
VARIETY OF WAYS TO MAKE HOMES
FOR THEMSELVES. HERE ARE
SOME OF THEM:

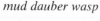
harvest mouse

cottontail rabbit

Learn Where Animals Live *(continued)*

logbook so you can keep a record of the homes you find.

What to Do: Note where homes are located: on ground, plants, shrubs, trees, under rocks, in caves. Try making sketches of the homes, or take pictures of them. Note the date when found, whether empty or occupied. If empty, try to figure out which animal built the home, and plan to go back next year to see if it's still there. Try to revisit several times, and watch the behavior of the occupant. Remember, don't collect bird nests. You can't always be sure the nest is deserted.

Certain types of insects' homes can be col-

lected; deserted wasp nests and spider webs, for instance.

Sometimes you'll find animals at work making homes—like a spider weaving a web. Some animals you'll learn about work at night, and if you ever camp near a colony of beavers, you might be able to watch one of these remarkable builders of dams and lodges at work. Take a flashlight, if there's no moonlight, and go quietly to the pond's edge. If you hear the busy beaver, flash the light in the direction of the sound. You'll have the thrill of your life watching this master engineer at work. Warning: Don't use the light too soon or you'll frighten him away.

mud dauber wasp   *gray fox*

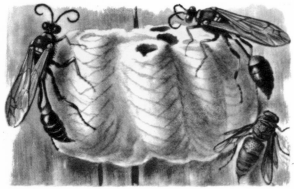

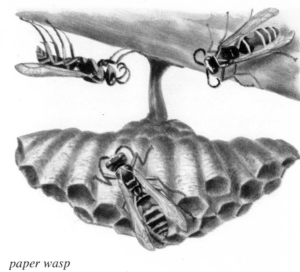

paper wasp

Baltimore oriole

hermit crab

muskrat

prairie dog

mole

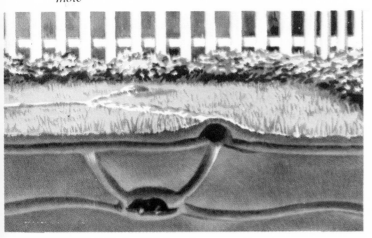

Eggshell Gardens

If you'd like to grow a window garden that looks as though it belonged in a "Hansel and Gretel" house, plant seeds or cuttings in eggshell pots, dyed when Easter eggs are dyed.

Choose large eggs. At the pointed ends, take off about one third of the shell by tapping eggs gently, picking shell off a little at a time, then dumping eggs out. Wash shells, inside and out. Dip gently into egg dye, then carefully crack the eggshells on the bottom to permit drainage.

Use aluminum foil to line each section of an egg carton, which you'll need to anchor wobbly pots. If you paint the egg carton, it will need two coats. Set garden in a sunny window. When plants outgrow pots, transplant to yard or flowerpots.

To Plant: Fill shells with sandy soil, leaving about ½ inch at the top to allow for watering. Sow just a few seeds in each, and cover with soil so as to barely conceal seeds. Knowing that you can transplant later on allows you a wide choice of seed to plant in these midget

Fill eggshells gently with dirt, taking care not to damage fragile shell.

A finished eggshell garden makes a colorful display.

pots. But make a note of what goes into each shell, so you'll be on speaking terms with what comes up. If you plant cuttings (3-inch ones of such house plants as geranium and begonia are easy to start with), stick the stems of these down almost to the bottom of the pots.

Water well, gently, and regularly after planting. After planting and watering seeds, cover pots with moist burlap, cloth, or newspaper, but remove cover as soon as plants start to sprout.

To Transplant: The time to do this is when the plants have outgrown their eggshell pots. If you transplant to clay pots, use standard 4-inch pots. Any smaller ones will be apt to make soil dry out too rapidly. In bottom of pot, lay in about 1½ inches of gravel, pebbles, or small pieces of broken flowerpots for drainage. Then put in about a ½ inch layer of peat or sphagnum moss to help hold moisture. This layer may be skipped, however, if the moss is not easy to come by.

Use good potting soil. If you live in the city where the soil is poor, buy it in small-sized bags from dime store or florist. Remove any stones or pebbles from soil, and mix two parts of dirt with one part humus.

In filling pots, press soil down with a stick or with the bottom of another pot until surface is ¾ inch below rim.

Now, you're ready to transfer seedlings from your eggshell garden into your specially prepared pots. When transplanting, first dig a hole for the plant, then carefully break the shell away from the lump of soil and roots, and set the plant down in the hole. Pack firmly.

As when they grew in eggshell pots, plants will continue to need water every day and will thrive best on the sunny side of the house.

To Transplant Out-of-doors: If you put seedlings into prepared ground, handle just as is suggested for pots. Most blooming yard plants like the sunny side of the house.

Whether in pots or in the yard, plants will thrive better if you'll cultivate the soil now and then—keep it from caking or hardening by poking gently, but not deeply, around the plants with a fork.

Make Seeds Sprout

Make a seed-observation lab, and from a front-row seat you'll see one of nature's most amazing spectacles. All you have to do is to sandwich dried seed between a wet blotter and glass. As tiny seed, seemingly lifeless, swell and first send out roots or a tangled mass of fuzz, then stems and leaves, you'll see the mystery of the continuation of plant life.

Here's the simple equipment you'll need for your experiment. Besides dried seeds—such as radish or bean, which are fast to sprout and easy to see—use several old water tumblers, or pieces of window glass, and some blotters. Old desk blotters may be used.

This experiment will enable you to watch seeds *sprout*. To *plant* seeds is another story. For that step, study directions on seed packages or ask help from the gardener in your family.

Preparing Dried Seed for Sprouting: There are two ways. For the water-tumbler method dried beans or corn, unpopped, may be used.

To prepare beans or corn for sprouting, soak seed overnight. Then put them at sides of tumbler, first lined with blotting paper cut to size. Try to place seed about halfway down sides of glass. Moisten blotter, and keep enough water in glass to cover lower half inch or so of blotter. Seed so prepared will burst in a couple of days, then begin to sprout.

The second way to sprout seed is the windowpane glass method, for which radish seed can be used very successfully. But radish seed don't need to be presoaked.

For this windowpane glass method, any size glass will do, but a piece 10 inches by 12 inches will be the handiest. You can use either two pieces of glass or one piece of glass and a cookie sheet or baking tin. Blotting paper, cut to size, is sandwiched in between the two.

Bean seeds sprout quickly when kept moist.

Place blotter on baking tin or piece of glass, dampen with water, sprinkle liberally with radish seed, then cover with a piece of glass. Moisten the blotter daily to keep it damp, and watch the seed as they begin to sprout. You'll see things happening in a couple of days.

What You'll See: In the bean, you'll first notice the lower part of the stem, or *hypocotyl,* break through the seed coat and turn downward. The upper stem and leaves, called *plumule,* push up.

The two halves of the bean seed, called *cotyledons*—which contain protein, starch, mineral matter, and water, as food—will push upward, spread apart, and turn green. These will gradually shrivel up as the green leaves develop and are ready to make their own food. This process of food making is called *photosynthesis*. By this time, the roots and root hairs are developed.

The corn seed, in contrast with the bean, has only one *cotyledon,* and it stays in place as the seed germinates. The food in the corn seed is stored inside it in a part called the *endosperm,* not in the *cotyledon* as in the bean.

In the radish, the seed bursts and sends forth the roots from the growing *hypocotyl.* The root hairs of the radish, just back of their growing tips, will appear as a mass of fuzz. Soon the stems and leaves will grow upward and, if a large number of seed has been placed on the blotter, will show their combined strength by actually pushing up the glass as they grow.

Collecting Seeds: Collecting seeds can be as much fun as making them sprout. To mount dried seeds for a collection, use cotton-lined cardboard boxes in sizes to house your specimens. For see-through windows in their lids, cut out openings and tape in glass or transparent plastic. Give each specimen a name tag.

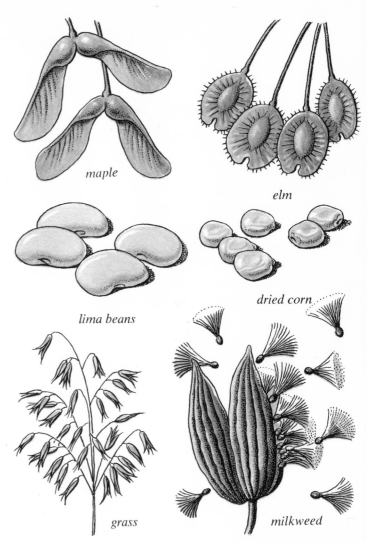

maple

elm

lima beans

dried corn

grass

milkweed

SOME EASY-TO-FIND SEEDS YOU CAN COLLECT

Line a glass with a blotter; put seed between the two. Keep moist and see what happens!

Cotton-lined boxes make a nice display case for dried seeds in see-through transparent envelopes.

Collecting Butterflies

Once you start collecting butterflies, you'll find you've also captured a key to the wonderland of insects and flowers. Butterflies sucking the sweet juices of lilacs and clover show the how-and-why of flowers' pollination. In the transformation from chrysalis into butterfly, you'll see one of nature's most spectacular displays.

All you need for this hobby is a net; "killing" jar; corrugated cardboard; tweezers or pinning forceps; paper strips; pins, for spreading; cotton and cigar box, for preserving treasures.

How to Make a Net: Sew about a square yard of mosquito netting into a cone-shaped bag. Then firmly sew the open end of it to a wire ring, made by shaping a wire coat hanger into a circle. To make a handle for the net, straighten out hook of hanger and lengthen it

by wiring securely to it a smooth piece of ½ inch dowel about 3 feet long.

To Use Carbon Tetrachloride Safely: Be very careful to keep face away from the fumes from the "killing" jar, which contains cotton wet with this dry-cleaning fluid. The purpose of this jar is to kill the butterflies painlessly.

Pin butterfly to board with paper strips.

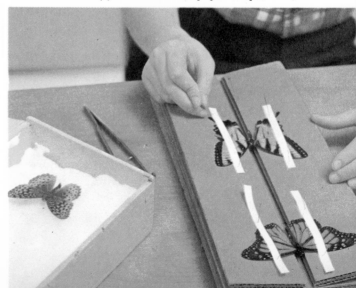

38

Always use jar outdoors or in a well-ventilated room, away from fire or open flame.

To Soften Stiffened Butterflies: If the specimens caught are left in storage envelopes long enough to stiffen, they'll need to be softened up before spreading. A widemouthed can or jar with a tightly fitting lid is ideal. Line the bottom with cotton, dampened with water. In these, specimens will soften overnight.

To Make a Spreading Board: This is made with a center channel into which to place the body of the butterfly. Sides of the board are slightly slanted toward this channel, so open wings can spread on the surface in a natural position.

Cut 6 pieces from a corrugated cardboard carton: two A pieces 10 inches by 20 inches; two B pieces 2 inches by 20 inches; two C pieces 4¾ inches by 20 inches.

Lay one A piece on top of the other, edges even. Around the edges, stick straight pins down through the two layers to hold them firmly together. Even with the side edges, lay the B pieces on top of A pieces, and stick pins down through outer edges to hold in place. Lay the C pieces on top of these, side edges even. Pin in place along all edges. This addition of the C pieces will make the center channel, ½ inch wide and about ¼ inch deep.

To Make Paper Strips: Cut heavy paper into strips about 1 inch by 3 inches. Pin strips in pairs to hold wings down to dry.

How to Spread Specimens: Using a pair of tweezers or pinning forceps, to prevent damage in handling, gently place the body of butterfly in the channel of the spreading board, and pin down through center of body. Spread wings one at a time; hold in place with paper strips by pinning strips at each end to the spreading board. Leave until dry, in a warm, airy place. This usually takes a couple of days. Then remove strips, and transfer specimens to a cotton-layered cigar box, for display.

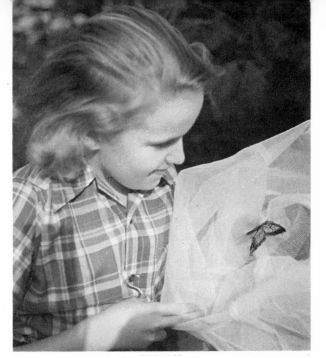

Open net carefully after catching butterfly.

Put butterfly in killing jar, quickly replace cover.

Place butterfly in envelope for carrying home.

39

Making A Desert Garden Indoors

You can learn secrets of the desert from a few pounds of gravel and sand, a nest of rocks, and some dry-land plants. If you admit animals into this little garden, another dimension of discovery is added. Habits of horned "toads" or other arid-land lizards, and of fleshy-stemmed cacti storing up moisture against desert droughts, reveal little miracles of life as eye-popping to watch as a Disney nature film.

In cultivating this garden, you'll learn to cut and plant succulent slips, and care for pets in an almost natural environment. Projects like this desert garden grown in a fish tank have sometimes led people into the faraway but rewarding field of horticulture.

Materials Needed: With the exceptions noted, the following materials can be bought from five-and-dime stores and pet shops.

Glass fish tank (any size, but 5-gallon size is the most practical); 4 or 5 pounds of gravel, obtained from gravelly roadsides, or perhaps from your own driveway (wash and dry gravel before using); ¼ pound charcoal, bought at a grocery store (put lumps or chunks in a cloth bag, and crush lightly with a hammer until it's fine); 2 pounds coarse sand; 2 pounds fine sand. If ocean-beach sand is used, it should first be thoroughly washed with fresh water and dried in the sun. Salt in sand may be bad for plants.

The desert plants (both spiny cacti and varieties of succulents, preferably in stair-step sizes) can be up to 7 or 8 inches tall. Cactus that blooms will make a more interesting garden.

One or two big rocks, or a nest of small ones, or pieces of weathered wood, are a nice addition. Good specimens can be found by the roadside.

For your animals, use horned toads and lizards. They make good pets. One of each makes an interesting pair.

Don't clutter your garden with too many plants. If it is too full, you won't be able to see the animals.

Tips on Planting: When planting, use blunt stick or spoon to push sand away while putting cactus in soil. To protect hands against spiny plants, wrap each plant in a piece of newspaper before handling. Try not to touch roots. And don't destroy root hairs. If there's any dirt hanging to roots, leave it on. Arrange plants so taller ones will be at rear of tank, shorter ones in front. Do not put plants too close to side of tank.

You'll be able to increase the succulents by cutting slips from growing specimens and planting. To cut a slip, simply select a leaf with a piece of stem. Plant as you did the "mother" plant. Water thoroughly after planting, but be very careful not to make the soil

Place finished desert garden by a sunny window.

40

Assemble all materials before starting to work. ▲   *Begin with a base of gravel, charcoal, and sand.* ▼

HORNED
Toads

Use a spoon to place plants in position.

A horned "toad" will thrive in your garden.

soggy. Put garden near window where it can get sunlight. Plants can take it full force, but animals will seek shelter from direct rays under nest of rocks, wood, or under the sand.

Watering Garden: A good watering once every two weeks is enough. Soil should dry out thoroughly between waterings.

Feeding Pets: Animals should be fed about once a week. They'll get water by licking it off plants. If you want to sink a dish of water into the sand, you can; but chances are your pets will use it as a bath.

Horned toads, which are really lizards, will eat ants. Best way to catch ants is to bait them with jam daubed on a piece of cardboard. Usually, leaving this bait on the ground will gather ants to the feast. If you can't get ants in the city, carry your bait to the park or nearby countryside. When the cardboard is lively with ants, drop it into a widemouthed jar, and cover.

At mealtime, lower the ant-infested cardboard into the tank. To keep ants from crawling out of tank, either cover it, while horned toad is eating, with a cut-to-size cardboard cover, or hand-feed your pet by giving him one ant at a time with a pair of tweezers.

To feed a lizard, get meal worms from a pet shop. For keeping a supply on hand, store worms in a tin can pierced with tiny holes. Pour some oatmeal into can for worms to eat; put in a piece of damp rag; cover can, and set it in a dark place.

Lizards also eat grasshoppers, which you'll have to catch in a net in a field or park. To feed a lizard grasshoppers or meal worms, dangle one in the tank on the end of a wire. Continue until the lizard stops eating, a sign he's had enough.

Gently spray water on garden every two weeks.

Use only dead or fallen branches when collecting specimens.

Collecting Wood Is Fun

Make a wood collection. There's no better way to make closer friends of trees, which are usually taken for granted as something to give shade, to bear fruit, or to climb.

But the minute you saw cuts into a branch (dead or fallen), you'll see a tree in a new light. The simple procedure of cutting into wood in order to prepare a specimen reveals texture in bark and grain as many-faceted as a jewel. When you shellac one half of the exposed area, to compare wood side by side in a natural and a finished state, you've made a good beginning in learning about that particular kind of tree.

Since there are 850 kinds of trees in the United States worth knowing, this hobby gives promise of many hours of pleasure!

You'll need a saw and vise, fine sandpaper, clear shellac and a small brush, and for labeling, paper, cellophane or sheet plastic, and some tacks.

Where to Collect: Never cut a living tree. The bark protects a tree from infection just as your skin protects you. A live tree may die from the wound inflicted by a boy or girl who saws off one small branch.

So, get your specimens from trees that have been cut or blown down. Quite often you'll find good pieces to collect which have been professionally trimmed from trees or which came from trees surrendered to the woodsman's ax in the process of building new roads or clearing land for new housing.

How to Collect: Look for branches on the ground that are at least 2 inches in diameter. Using a saw, cut off a straight piece of branch about 10 inches long, trying to cut where the bark is in good condition. Before you leave with your branch, note for your records these characteristics of the tree from which it comes: shape of tree, leaves, and fruit, if any. If the

43

Place wood in vise before sawing.

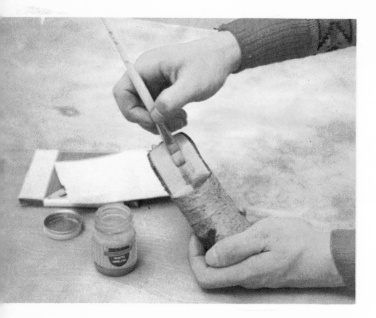

Shellac one half of the exposed area of the wood.

Collecting Wood Is Fun *(continued)*

wood isn't fairly well dried out when you get your specimen home, put it in a warm place to dry. Green branches may take several weeks to dry.

How to Prepare Collection: Take the 10-inch length of wood and fasten horizontally in a vise. Using a piece of cloth to protect bark from scratch marks is a good idea, especially if the wood is very soft. Now, you're all set to make the important five cuts into the wood, using these steps:

1. Saw off one end as squarely as you can. After measuring off 7 inches of length, saw off other end.

2. Placing the block upright in the vise, saw down through the center 3½ inches, or half way.

3. With the block still upright, saw across to the halfway point where the wood has been cut vertically. This will cut free a section of wood; remove it.

4. Now, at the top half of the specimen cut off another section, this time a diagonal slice slanted down at a 45-degree angle.

5. Remove from vise and sandpaper all cut areas smooth, sanding with the grain. If sandpaper is wrapped around a small squared-off block of wood, you'll do a better job of keeping wood surfaces smooth.

To Shellac: Lightly pencil a line lengthwise through center of cut areas, dividing them in two equal parts. Shellac only one half of each area, using a small brush. This will enable you to see how wood looks in both natural and finished state.

How to Label Collection: On each specimen attach a label on which the name of the tree is printed. A piece of white paper 1 inch by 3 inches and a protective cover of cellophane or clear plastic, cut the same size, can be fastened to the specimen with two small tacks.

How to House Collection: Specimens can be stored in a large cardboard box or in a bureau drawer. But since they're fun to display for friends to admire or study, it's better if you can build some small open shelves, divided into compartments, say 3 inches by 8 inches in size. Specimens can also be displayed by hanging—by using screw eye and hook—from the bottom of a wall shelf if it is strong and solidly hung. Put screw eyes in the tops of specimens, hooks along the bottom of shelf.

44

A shadow box with many compartments will make a handsome showcase for your best specimens.

Friendly Fellows In Your Garden

Welcome to your garden any animal that'll help keep it from becoming an open-air cafeteria for hungry insects. Earthworms won't repel hungry hordes, but they're the best plowmen in the animal world. So, hang out the welcome sign for them. Also for bees. Both honeybees and bumblebees will do a job of fertilization while buzzing from flower to flower.

These so-called green-thumbed animals willingly work all summer long, and without pay. They require no upkeep. They ask for no vacation. If your garden lacks valuable helpers, you can lure or bring them into your flower plot or vegetable patch. Birds can be encouraged to come if you'll put out bird-houses and birdbaths. You can import from the nearby countryside many animals whose value to a garden is described in detail below.

The Toad: Fastened to the front of his mouth is a formidable weapon—his long sticky tongue. Flipped out to snare a bug, cutworm, or any other hapless creature, it's whipped back quick as a flash with the prey he's trapped. There's an old wives' tale that says toads cause warts, but doctors pooh-pooh this superstition. Don't drive this bug catcher from your garden.

The Earthworm: A great tunneler whose lips are his digging tools. He swallows soil as he burrows through it, leaves it behind him softer and finer. Through his tunnels air flows to

WELCOME THESE HELPFUL TENANTS TO YOUR GARDEN

bees

birds

green snake

praying mantis

toad

earthworm

ladybugs

Toads help get rid of unwanted bugs by eating them.

Earthworms burrow through soil, leaving it softer.

roots of plants, helps to keep the soil sweet.

Ladybird Beetle: Sometimes called ladybug or lady beetle, this garden helper (in its larval form) feeds on plant lice or aphids that suck plants dry. The female beetle lays her eggs on leaves that are well covered with aphids. The eggs hatch out into hungry larvae which soon devour the harmful aphids. California fruit-growers use ladybird beetles to control scale insects, a first cousin of the aphid.

Praying Mantis: From the time he hatches in May until he's full grown in August this ferocious friend of the garden feeds on insects that threaten plant life. The inch-long egg mass from which baby praying mantes emerge is attached to a plant stem. If you'd like several hundred active vigilantes for garden work next May or June, look for an egg mass in the woods in the fall, snip off the plant stem on which it's attached, and set it up to hatch in the family vegetable patch or flower plot.

The Bee: If you have fruit trees in your garden, both domestic honeybees and wild bumble-bees will pollinate the flowers. Carrying fine yellow or white dust on his legs, the bee fertilizes plants as he flies from one flower to another.

The Green Snake: Destroyer of caterpillars, grasshoppers, crickets, and other insect pests, the small, slender green snake which slithers away at your approach deserves your friendliest overtures. He is completely harmless.

Birds: The wren, chickadee, brown thrasher, cuckoo, and countless more birds relentlessly devour caterpillars, leaf hoppers, wireworms, grasshoppers, and other harmful insects. For names of many feathered friends that will come in and help out in the garden, study books about birds to discover which ones live in your part of the country.

47

How To Grow A Crystal Garden

Crystals of minerals make some of the most beautiful structures found in nature. They range from the lacy crystals of fleeting snow-flakes to the carbonized crystals of lasting diamonds. No matter how short-lived or enduring, such crystals show what a wonderful chemist nature is. Fascinated by her creations, most people want to know how they're formed. If you're one of those, you can make a small-size marvel of your own, right in your own kitchen. The crystals you make will keep on growing for several days and will last for weeks. Although this will be a small adventure into the wondrous realm of crystals, it can lead to much bigger things. A crystal garden is certain to pull you and your curiosity farther into the fascinating field of chemistry.

Equipment: To grow a crystal garden you'll need the following items: A common brick, soft coal, or coke; plain salt; household ammonia; liquid bluing; coloring; a hammer (an old one will do); dishes (several of the bowl or dish type about 6 inches in diameter); bowl, pitcher, or empty can for mixing ingredients; medicine dropper; tablespoon; water.

The coloring matter called for can be either food coloring, mercurochrome, or fabric dye.

Preparing the Garden: With hammer, break brick, soft coal, or coke into small pieces about the size of large walnuts. Place several of these in one dish. Don't overcrowd the dish, and be sure, when arranging pieces, to cluster them right in the center of it. This way, when crystals begin to grow, they aren't so apt to spill over the sides.

Now assemble the rest of the ingredients and mix them together in the following order. This will give you a mixture sufficient for one 6-inch dish: 4 tablespoons plain common salt (it must not be iodized); 4 tablespoons liquid bluing; 4 tablespoons water; 1 tablespoon household ammonia.

Pour this mixture very slowly over the broken pieces clustered in the dish. Then, with the medicine dropper filled first with one color, then the next that you want to use (rinsing dropper between changes of color), give your creation its technicolor brilliance by dropping small amounts of coloring over the rock pile in the dish.

The Garden's Growth: In a short time, little crystals will begin to form. Within a few hours after "planting," garden will begin to take on odd and interesting shapes.

How To Display Your Garden: Plan to exhibit it close to where you drop on the final coloring. Because it can crumble at a touch, don't risk this by moving it about too much.

Pour liquid mixture slowly over pieces of brick.

Crystal gardens are fragile. Handle with care.

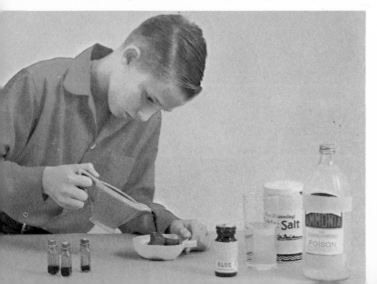

Make your own star box and learn about the constellations.

Stargazing

The best way to explore the mysteries of the skies is to star hop. Start with one star group you already recognize, the Big Dipper, for instance, and work your way around the night sky. Amateur excursions into the realm of astronomy can teach you a great deal about a science which has fascinated man for thousands of years.

All the equipment you need to make astronomy your hobby is good eyesight, a library book on stars that has a simple chart of the constellations (star groups), and a pair of inexpensive low-power field glasses.

If you live near a planetarium, one of those exciting theaters of the heavens, you'll find it a wonderful place to go to study star formations. But if you don't live near one, you can build a star box, a miniature planetarium of your own. All you'll need is an ordinary box (a shoebox will do nicely), black paint, a flashlight, and some slides perforated to give you the same star patterns that are found in the sky.

The perforated black slides inserted into the star box and lighted by the flashlight will give the illusion of star patterns found in a

49

Ursa Major (Big Dipper)

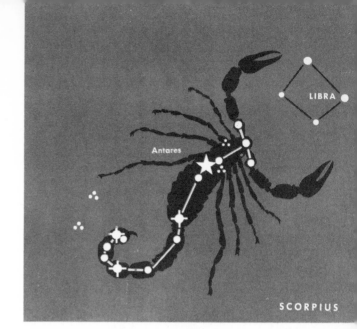

Scorpius

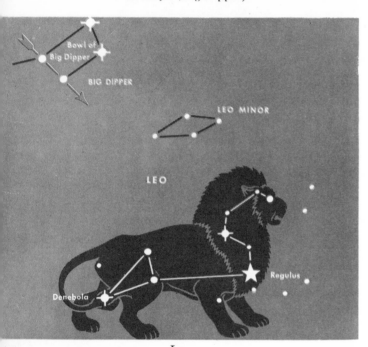

Leo

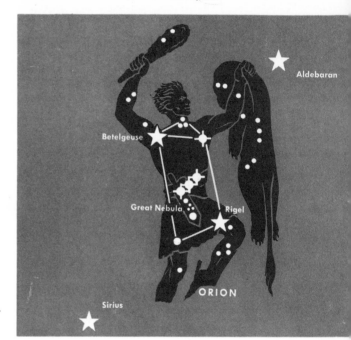

Orion

Pegasus

Cygnus

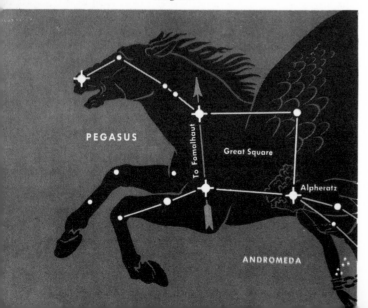

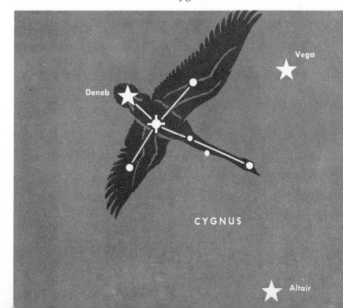

night sky. The purpose of this is to teach yourself to recognize the star groupings in various constellations. Stars are suns, and are traveling through space, although not all in the same direction. Star patterns (constellations) as we now see them will change eventually. This won't happen in our lifetime, but as time goes on.

There are about 88 constellations in all, but you can begin your star study with nine. Start with three all-year-round constellations: Big Dipper, Little Dipper, and Cassiopeia (Queen's Chair); three which appear in the winter: Canis Major (Big Dog), Orion (Mighty Hunter) and Taurus (Bull); three seen in spring and summer: Leo (Lion), Hercules, Scorpius (Scorpion).

Directions: Measure, then pencil a ¾-inch margin around top of box cover. Cut along line, leaving ¾-inch frame. Cut out nine cardboard slides for the constellations listed. Make slide same dimensions as inside of box cover. Apply one coat of black paint to outside of box, and to both sides of each slide. Following constellation charts and using a medium size nail, punch through holes in slide for each star in a given group. Also cut out a hole to insert head of flashlight, at one side of box.

◄ *Use these pictures of constellations to make slides for your star box.*

HOW TO USE THE BIG DIPPER TO STAR HOP ►

First find the seven bright stars which form the Big Dipper. Four stars form the bowl of the dipper, three the handle. To locate the bright star Arcturus in the constellation Boötes just follow the curved handle of the dipper out from the bowl, continue in that direction and the first bright star you come to will be Arcturus. To find Polaris, the North Star, use the two stars which form the side of the bowl of the Big Dipper away from the handle. These are called the pointers. Extend an imaginary line connecting these two stars and extend that line in the direction of the opening of the bowl about five times its length. The star you find will be Polaris. Now you can find the rest of the Little Dipper as Polaris is at the end of its handle.

How to Begin: Use your star box as a help in searching the heavens for the real thing. Have field glasses and constellation chart with you, also flashlight for checking chart from time to time.

Which Stars to Study First? Suppose you start with the Big Dipper, always in our starlit northern sky. Notice the four stars that form the bowl and the three that make the curved handle. Go next to the Little Dipper, nearby, and shaped like it. The star in the very end of the curved handle is the North Star. Known also as Polaris, it is almost directly above the north geographic pole of the earth, and sailors and travelers have for centuries used it as a guide to tell which way was North.

Now, you might look for Orion, the Mighty Hunter. You'll recognize him by his belt, a row of three stars. Study his belt through your field glasses, and then try to locate the bright star, Betelgeuse, that marks Orion's shoulder.

Search for Rigel, Orion's left leg, and for the fainter stars forming his club. Following the belt stars upward, you'll find the constellation group known as Taurus. Aldebaran, the liveliest star, is the eye of the bull.

With these star hops as a beginning, go on to locate others. As the seasons change, make other star groups the destination for exciting space travels.

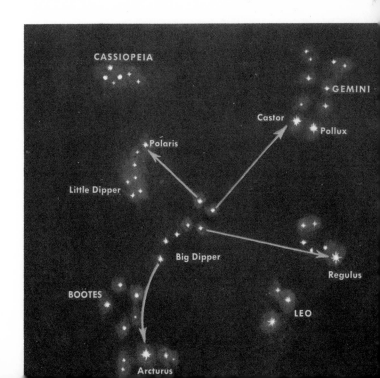

Let's Go Nutting

Besides the fun of filling your sack and having a feast from it, you can pick up some interesting facts about the specimens you gather when you go on a nutting hike.

Nuts are fruits of certain trees. Even hard-shelled nuts like walnuts belong to the same big family of fruits as apples, pears, cherries, and plums. But a walnut differs from its fleshy first cousins in being a dry fruit, having a hard hull, and containing only one seed. On these single seeds the generations of walnut and other trees-to-come depend.

Like all fruits, nuts appear first on trees as flowers. Some of these are quite beautiful in their shaggy, burr-like, or fuzzy clusters. From flower to woody bract which, formed in layers, makes a hard- or soft-shelled cup, capsule, hull, or husk, is the process of nut development.

Because, strictly speaking, the nut is a fruit, the delicious kernel you dig out of the shell to eat is a seed.

To find out for yourself just how talented nature is as a nut designer, saw a few specimens in two. Place a walnut, pecan, hickory, or other hard-shelled nut in a vise and saw it

down the middle, and you'll be able to study the variety of patterns found in nuts. Structures range from simple designs like that of the acorn to many curved mazes within woody compartments, like that of the hickory nut. You'll discover details of construction, even when some nuts are stripped of kernels, as intricate as the work of a fine cabinetmaker.

While you're learning interesting facts about nuts, you may like to know that some take faraway trips into the world of trade. Although they won't be the ones you'll find in the woods when you go out to shake trees, some nuts are valuable for making oil, soap, paints, varnishes, cigarette holders, and even buttons.

But because our country is blessed with a fine array of nut-bearing trees, there are many you will find when you head for the country.

The Art of Finding Edible Nuts: October and November are the best months. The ideal time is after a heavy windstorm when, if you're a jump ahead of the squirrels and chipmunks, you'll find nuts plentifully strewn on the ground beneath the trees. Learning to recognize nut trees by the leaves and bark will add to your knowledge of trees.

A small, slender nut-bearing tree can be shaken to break loose some of the nuts. You may need to use a long stick to shake nuts loose from low hanging branches, a short stick for tossing into the tree to make higher ones topple. Not all edible nuts grow on tall trees; some, like hazelnuts and the delicious pine nuts of the Southwest, are often within arm's reach. You may need a hammer to crack open some of the harder nuts you find. Most nuts are tastier after they've been allowed to dry and season for awhile. If picked while hulls are green, put in a sunny spot to dry. Toasting or roasting and salting nut meats usually improves their flavor.

A small stick thrown into a nut tree will send down a shower of nuts.

Edible American Nuts: Depending upon the locality you live in, here are nuts that are yours for the finding.

Hickories: Not all hickory nuts are good to eat. The bitternut isn't. Best and sweetest among the edible hickories are the shagbark and the big shellbark. The shellbark has a larger hull than the shagbark but the meat is small, isn't as tasty.

The pecans, prizes among hickories, are found in the South and some areas of the East. Their meats are hard to dig out, but are worth the effort.

Walnuts: Black walnuts, found in the eastern half of the country, are not too common because so many of the trees have been cut for wood. But their meats are a delicacy. They're oily, though, so don't eat too many at one time. Many nut gatherers spread these, while hulls are a smooth yellow, on woodshed roof or other roof to dry until they're black so that they'll be easier to shuck.

The English walnuts, found in the South and in California, are grown commercially for their nut meats, which in thin shells are easy to extract.

Butternuts: Also called white walnuts, they are found in the East and Northeast. Delicious table relishes to eat with meats are sometimes made of these. A very old recipe calls for gathering while the butternut hulls are green, rubbing off their soft fuzz, scalding the nuts—hull and all—in boiling water, then pickling in spiced vinegar.

Hickories, cut crosswise, reveal marvelous patterns.

Beechnuts: Because they're small and covered with a thin, leathery shell, some people don't bother to extract their meats. But they're very good and have a rich, delicate flavor.

Pine nuts: In the Southwest, these nuts—actually large wingless seeds—gathered from cones of the piñon pine are favorites. Easy to gather, they can be shaken from open cones.

Chestnuts: The *edible* chestnut is scarce because a blight killed off many trees. When found, this nut is delicious—more so, if roasted. The plentiful horse chestnut is, however, *inedible*.

Hazelnuts: Grown on shrubs and easily gathered, hazelnuts (or filberts) are often found along roads. These are the small, native hazelnuts. The larger ones we buy are imported.

SOME EASY-TO-FIND NUTS TO GATHER

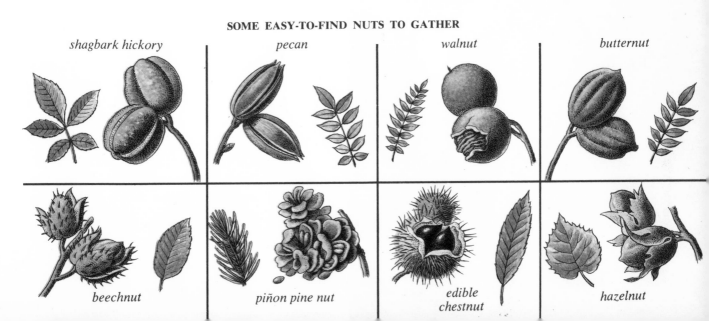

shagbark hickory   pecan   walnut   butternut

beechnut   piñon pine nut   edible chestnut   hazelnut

Play Santa To Your Bird Friends

Foraging for bugs and seeds in dead of winter is tough going for birds. Share your holiday bounty—fruits, nuts, popcorn—and your fun will be in watching these hungry friends enjoy a feast. For a small outlay spent for a chunk of suet, sunflower seeds, ears of dried wheat or corn, and paper cups for baskets to hang food on a tree, you can throw quite a party for your bird friends. The tree can be an evergreen growing in the yard or lower boughs cut from your Christmas tree, stuck in the ground or window box.

You may become so interested in your hobby that, in time, you'll go even further and plant bushes that bear edible berries, and cultivate sunflowers, whose seeds birds like.

No Fancy Diet Is Needed: Birds will like fat trimmings from meat and bones as much as a chunk of suet you might buy. Any dried seed from weeds you find growing can be hung on the tree. Birds like peanuts in and out of shells. A little peanut butter mixed with crumbs is another treat you can add to the cranberries, nut meats, popcorn (popped), apple slices, suet, and other party fare put in

Trim tree with good things for birds to eat.

Some birds like suet, stuffed into pine cones.

Bluejays and sparrows are among the many birds that will visit your festive tree.

paper cups. To hang apple slices, push a wire hairpin—or small piece of wire—halfway into slice; tie ribbon to protruding loop. Tiny chunks of suet rolled in bird seed can be individually tied with ribbons or cord.

Even in colder regions, water put in a shallow dish under the tree won't freeze too fast for birds to drink it, if it's a mild day.

To Outwit Unwanted Guests: If rabbits, squirrels, or other unwanted guests crash your party, you can keep them from raiding refresh-ments by hanging food on long strings, well away from other branches. This, in particular, is a clever way to outwit squirrels. Also, paper cups containing food can be covered with lids of ½-inch wire mesh (available at hardware stores) which will allow birds to poke their bills in but keep interlopers out. Using an old pair of scissors or tin snips, cut wire-mesh rounds just large enough to push down into paper cups and lodge there. Before filling and covering cups, stuff bottoms with paper to raise food to the mesh.

Squirrels and other animals will visit tree, too. To protect food for birds, hang on high branches.

Pound leaf with old shoe brush to expose veins.

Leaf skeletons can be kept between sheets of glass.

black oak

Making Leaf Skeletons

Stripping green leaves down to their skeletons introduces you to one of nature's greatest wonders. When you pound away the fleshy parts of a leaf you'll discover the delicate veins that plants use to carry the raw materials they make into food. Through these lacelike life lines the food passes on to nourish other parts of the plant.

To Skeletonize a Leaf: Besides the fresh green leaf, you'll need an old hairbrush or shoebrush with animal bristles, fairly fine but not stiff (nylon or other synthetic bristles are too harsh), and a "pounding board." You can make the board by tacking a piece of old carpeting about 8 inches by 10 inches on top of a plank.

Put leaf on board, top side up, hold firmly in place with one hand, and tap gently until

sweet gum

red maple

all the fleshiness is worn away, leaving only the skeleton of veins. Every once in a while turn leaf over and tap its underside. After 10 minutes or so, hold leaf to the light to see what progress you're making.

To Preserve Leaf Skeletons: You can mount in a scrapbook, glue to a single piece of window-pane glass or, to keep for longer duration, place leaf skeletons between two sheets of glass. To attach to the pages of a scrapbook, lay skeleton flat, cover with piece of cellophane and fasten with bits of transparent adhesive tape. To mount on a single sheet of glass, use a few dabs of clear plastic cement on the back of leaf skeleton along center rib and a couple of main branches.

To preserve between sheets of glass of equal size, lay specimens flat on one in whatever arrangement you like and top with the other. Fasten the two sheets firmly together all around the edges with adhesive tape. Add identifying label before taping together.

The leaf "factory" that you have uncovered has earned this nickname because it manufactures food for both plants and animals. Since animals can't make sugar, starch, fats, or vita-

mins out of water, gas, and minerals, green plants perform this magic for them in their leaf factories. The plants take up these substances in mineral-laden water. This nourishing fluid seeps up through cells of tiny but vital root hairs located at the ends of plant roots. Water passes up through ducts in the stem or trunk of a plant or tree until it finally reaches the leaves where it flows to all parts through the network of veins.

Meanwhile, certain specialized leaf cells take in carbon dioxide from the air. By means of chlorophyll, a very important substance in the leaf which gives plants their green coloring, the carbon dioxide and water are brought together and form sugar. Sunlight provides the energy for the chemical reaction that produces the sugar—so sun is the power that runs the leaf factory. When sugar is formed, it is carried through the ducts to other parts of the plant. Some of it, however, is changed into starch, and is stored in roots, seeds, and stems.

But that's not all of the amazing things a leaf does. It throws off waste products—water and oxygen. The oxygen—we all know how important it is—returns to the air and is used by other living things.

Where Do Animals Go In Winter?

Today, even children know better than did the ancients who believed that animals vanished magically in winter and popped up just as mysteriously in the spring. But if you want to find out where your forest friends go, take a walk in the woods and look around you.

Tiny tracks in fresh snow are apt to prove that squirrels and rabbits are around, foraging for food. Poke around old rotted logs, and you'll see the winter homes of many insects. Cocoons hanging from tree branches will be the winter sleeping bags of some beautiful moths-to-be.

By simply following your own curiosity around, you can study the three marvelous systems for survival different creatures use. One fascinating device of many birds is migration, which means going to warmer climes, like lucky people taking off to lands of sunshine and palms. Another is adaptation, an animal's way of changing into heavier furs or cleverly camouflaging the color of his coat for better protection. But most interesting is hibernation, for which the Rip Van Winkles of the animal world go into a deep sleep until spring, quite oblivious to bad weather, cheerless quarters, scant food supplies, or constant threats of hungry enemies.

Here are the winter-survival methods of some of our more familiar creatures:
Mammals: Some, like the rabbit, fox, weasel, bobcat, and squirrel grow a heavier coat of fur. The weasel's coat becomes white; blending in with the snow, it fools his enemies and also his prey. Other mammals hibernate in caves, burrows, and even barns. Seven of these, known as "the seven sleepers" are: the little brown bat, skunk, chipmunk, black bear, jumping mouse, woodchuck, and raccoon. Some prepare for winter a long time before it comes, by feasting heavily through the late summer months in order to fatten up for hibernation.

Add to mammals those which stay active all winter and continue to live in their all-year-round homes: deer, moles, marten, mink,

Turtles head for ponds when winter comes.

Bats hibernate in barns, caves, and attics.

otter, fox, beaver, field mice, and porcupine.

Birds: Bobolinks, among the first to fly south, gather into flocks by mid-July. Many others migrate south, but their place is taken by winter residents flying down from the colder north to winter with us.

Fresh-water Fish: Many move to deeper water in lakes and ponds. Trout, for one, move to flowing streams which remain open all winter. Although it can't definitely be said any of our native fish hibernate, some become quite sluggish in winter.

Crayfish: Some dig into burrows below frost line or down to ground water. Some lie in a stupor under stones.

Turtles: They hibernate in various places, depending upon species; some in the mud of lake, stream, pond bottoms; others burrow into the ground.

Bullfrogs: They hibernate from September to May in muddy ooze of pond bottom.

American Toads: They hibernate in soft soil, from a few inches deep to as much as 4 feet down under, often in gardens.

Salamanders: Many survive in adult form in streams and brooks or skulking beneath stones.

Snails: Land snails hibernate under stones, bury themselves under moss, leaves, or earth. Pond snails migrate from shallow to deeper water, to a depth of about 20 feet.

Spiders: They winter in all stages: as adults hiding in sheltered places; as spiderlings hatched but safe and protected within the egg sac. Other species remain in egg stage.

Earthworms: They hibernate 3 to 6 feet below the surface of ground.

Insects: The life cycle of some spans the winter. Among many types, however, only females survive to carry on the species. In some cases, both parents die, and offspring survive in eggs or pupae.

Among moths and butterflies, although some migrate, many others see winter through in a dormant stage, as caterpillars or as pupae in chrysalises or cocoons. Sometimes they survive the winter in the egg stage.

Katydids also survive by means of eggs laid in the summer.

Beetles seek the shelter of dried cornstalks, evergreen buds, and crotches of trees, rotting logs, and hiding places on the ground. Ladybugs in the East like to winter in old-fashioned attics.

THINGS TO SEE AND DO ON A WINTER HIKE

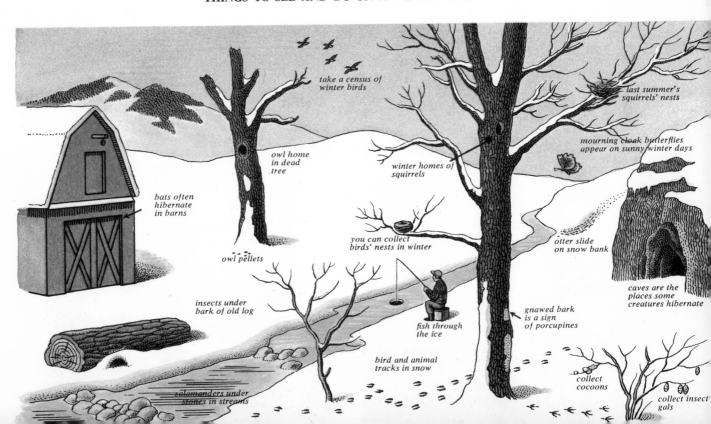

take a census of winter birds

last summer's squirrels' nests

mourning cloak butterflies appear on sunny winter days

owl home in dead tree

winter homes of squirrels

bats often hibernate in barns

you can collect birds' nests in winter

otter slide on snow bank

owl pellets

caves are the places some creatures hibernate

insects under bark of old log

fish through the ice

gnawed bark is a sign of porcupines

bird and animal tracks in snow

collect cocoons

salamanders under stones in streams

collect insect galls

Tropical Fish

An interesting indoor hobby, especially if you have a curious mind, is to start your own aquarium of tropical fish. With a pair of Mexican swordtails and a pair of rainbow-striped guppies, you will be able to study the feeding, fighting, mating, and breeding habits of these tiny denizens of southern waters. Tropical fish fanciers spend hundreds of dollars on this hobby, but you can start for about $5.00.

What you will need, first of all, is a tank. Buy a rectangular one which holds 2½ or 3½ gallons. Start with a pair of hardy tropical live-bearing fish like guppies, platies, or a pair of colorful Mexican swordtails. To help supply your pets with oxygen and to give them something to dart behind when they want to hide, buy about six plants. Some plants have to be planted, like the arrowheads and the eel-grasses, and some are free-floating, such as the fanwort and the hornwort. Finally, buy a ½ pound of sand or gravel.

Before laying in the gravel (not beach sand,

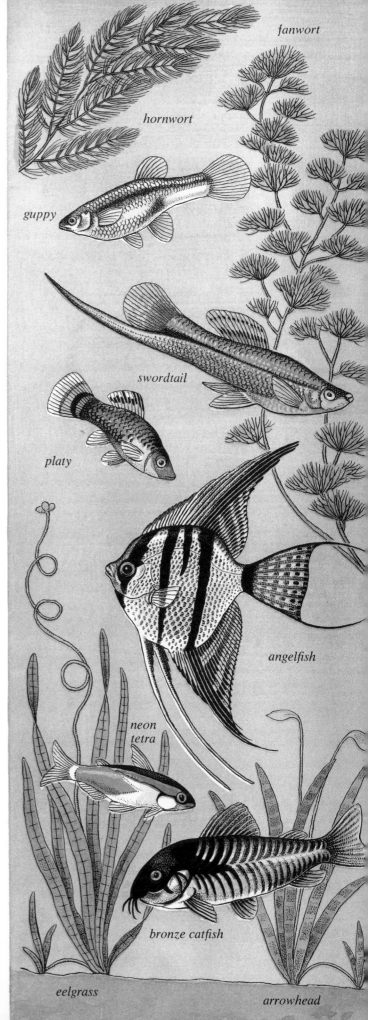

guppy

hornwort

fanwort

swordtail

platy

angelfish

neon tetra

bronze catfish

eelgrass

arrowhead

which would be harmful), wash it under running water. Anchor the rooted plants, and bank the sand so that it slopes from ½-inch in the front of the tank to 1 inch in the back. Add water and let the tank stand a few days before putting in your fish.

A temperature of 70 to 75 degrees is best. A 10-watt bulb suspended over the water, or a standard aquarium reflector used over the tank, will maintain the correct temperature. Light is essential, but more than two hours a day of direct sunlight may make your aquarium green with an overgrowth of plants.

Feeding is easy. Once a day gently sprinkle a little food onto the water. If the fish eat this, add a little more but be careful. Overfeeding is a common, and fatal, mistake.

If your aquarium is properly set up you won't have to change the water. Water will evaporate so you will have to add a little from time to time. Pour it in slowly.

Don't be surprised if a pair of live-bearing guppies proudly present you with fifteen baby guppies in one blessed event. Remove the little ones to a "nursery" jar of water until it's safe for a few of them to rejoin the family, usually after two weeks. (Hungry guppy parents have been known to eat their young!) You can swap or sell the other baby guppies to friends, and thus add to your own collection.

Build And Fill An Insect Zoo

Starting off with a praying mantis, a cricket, and a couple of small cages, you can set up a table-top zoo. As you become more ambitious, you can expand it.

Believing that crickets bring good luck, the Chinese for centuries have kept them as pets, often housing them in exquisite cages of gourd, bamboo, and jade. You may not expect your insects to bring you good luck, but you *can* expect them to give you hours of pleasure and the opportunity to study some of nature's remarkable creatures.

Their feeding habits, their unique ways of adapting themselves to various kinds of environments, their almost magic-like transformation from egg to adult, will all serve to make insect study a fascinating pastime for you, your family, and your friends.

Most of the equipment you'll need can be made or found at home. What can't be, is inexpensive to buy.

Equipment: Butterfly net for catching specimens; glass jars with lids—for carrying specimens and live food home; umbrella and a stick (about 3 feet long, 1 inch thick) for beating bushes for live food; cages; dirt for some cages.

An assortment of homemade cages is the best way to exhibit your private zoo.

To make a butterfly net, sew 1 square yard mosquito netting into cone-shaped bag. Sew open end to a ring (wire coat hanger shaped into circle). Straighten out hook of hanger; wire it securely to a stick 3 feet long.

Cages: 1. Pint and quart jars with tiny holes punched in screw-on lids. 2. Oil-lamp globe or chimney, set in small flowerpot, or coffee can, half-filled with dirt; cover chimney with fine screening. 3. Cardboard box with hole cut in lid (cover hole with a piece of clear plastic, attach with rubber cement), flap door cut in back through which to put food and water (seal door with adhesive tape to keep shut), tiny holes punched in one side of box for ventilation. 4. "Glass" houses made from 6 photographic slides cut about 3¼ inches square or window glass or clear sheet plastic cut to any convenient size. Tape sides of 5 pieces of glass together to make open-top box; tape sixth piece along one edge to make hinged lid. Use toothpick to prop lid up a crack to admit air.

Collecting Live Food: Easiest place to forage is where there are shrubs or bushes. Hold open umbrella upside down under a bush; beat branches with stick. Into jar scoop tiny insects that drop into umbrella; screw on lid.

Use ventilated jars for carrying specimens home.

grasshopper

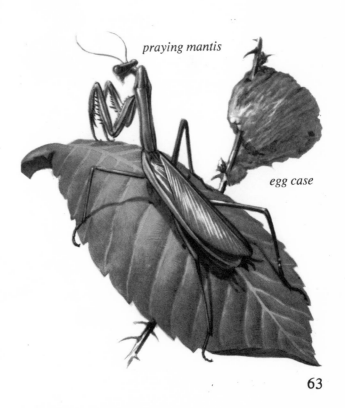

praying mantis

egg case

63

Cecropia larva

Cecropia cocoon

Cecropia moth

Food and Care: Once-a-day-feeding is usually enough, but don't worry about overfeeding. Most insects will eat any time you feed them but will stop when they've had enough. For the first few typical insect specimens you collect, here are simple tips on care.

Praying Mantes: Feed them flies, small insects. Sometimes they will feed on bits of raw chopped meat or liver, served on tip of toothpick. Keep mantis egg mass, collected in fall or winter, in a cage until the young emerge.

Field Crickets: Fill bottom of cage with an inch or so of soil; set some bottle caps into soil, and keep filled with water. Feed crickets bits of bread soaked in water, dabs of mashed potato, lettuce, peanut butter.

Click Beetles: Feed them soft-bodied insects, meal worms. Keep a water dish in the cage.

Grasshoppers, Walking Sticks: Put a small piece of grass sod into cage; water grass from time to time. Grass provides food; females can deposit eggs in the soil. Add dish of water.

Caterpillars: Always feed them leaves from the same kind of plant on which you found them. Give them this fare until they stop eating and enter the chrysalis or cocoon stage to become butterflies or moths.

walkingstick

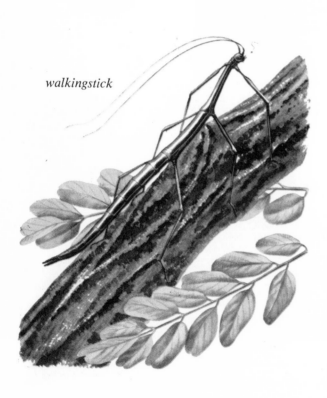

katydids

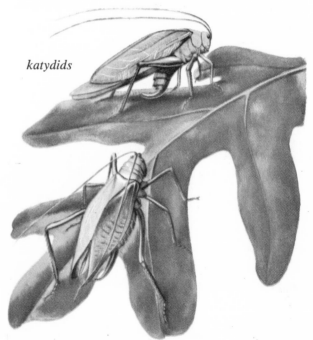

*After you've established your zoo, you can collect tiny insects to feed
your animals by beating the shrubbery with a stick over an open umbrella.*

Butterflies And Moths
Are Nature's Cinderellas

Butterflies leaving their hard-skinned little capsules called chrysalids, and moths their dried cocoons, to fly into a world of sun and flowers are like the beautiful princess of the fairy tale, freed from an evil enchantment. If you want to be an eyewitness to this transformation, collect chrysalids or cocoons, or both; place them in a jar or fish tank; see that they have enough moisture; and wait for them to hatch. In a "nursery" kept indoors, they may hatch from two weeks to a month earlier than if kept outdoors.

Besides jar or tank, the equipment you'll need will be an old cigar box, or cardboard box of similar size, penknife, notebook, and pencil.

Where to Look: Chrysalids and cocoons are found almost everywhere. To be successful in your search, you need keen eyesight and persistence. Look on leaves and branches of trees and shrubs. Search the thickets and brushwood. Look inside barns and garages, along fences and fence-posts, window sills, under stones, among dead leaves and even in topsoil, particularly during garden-digging time.

When to Look: Any time during the year. Those hanging from branches are most easily seen when trees are bare of leaves.

How to Collect: Carry box, penknife, notebook, and pencil with you. Handle the chrysalid or cocoon gently, so as not to damage the creature inside. If it's hanging to a tree, cut off the twig, leaving about 5 or 6 inches of twig still attached to the cocoon. This will make it easier to handle.

Place cocoon (the same applies to chrysalids) in your box, and continue looking for others. In your notebook write where you

found the cocoon. Later on, when it hatches, you can write down name of moth or butterfly. This record will be your guide to good locations in your next year's cocoon-search.

Testing a Cocoon: To see if the pupa inside is alive, shake it gently. If it rattles dryly, the pupa is probably dead; if there's a dull bump against the cocoon, the pupa is alive. If the cocoon is very light, and has a hole in it, that's proof the moth or butterfly has already emerged.

How to Raise Butterflies and Moths from Chrysalids and Cocoons: Use glass jars with wide openings, covered with pierced lids or cloth netting; or better still, a fish tank with screen or glass top. If using a glass top, prop it so as to admit air. Leave cocoons on twigs, if that's the way you found them, or hang up by tying with a thread to twig or branch, or lay

From this unattractive cocoon will emerge . . .

them on bottom of jar or tank. Branch or twig will also give the butterfly or moth something to cling to when ready to emerge. If you use a tank, floor it with sand or moss.

If you keep the container outdoors, put it in a sheltered spot, such as open porch or stoop. If indoors, keep it away from direct sunlight. Indoors, you will have to supply moisture if a jar is used. A wet blotter, or a piece of wet sponge from which water has been squeezed, placed on the bottom of the "nursery" will keep the cocoon from drying out. Don't lay the cocoon on the damp blotter or sponge. When blotter or sponge becomes dry —check daily—wet again.

If you use a tank, sprinkle a little water on the moss every few days. Be careful not to soak the cocoon.

Butterflies and moths have four completely different stages of life—egg, larva, pupa, and adult form.

Starting as tiny eggs deposited along the underside of a twig, or on a leaf, they pass through three more stages, climaxing in the most beautiful of all, the adult butterfly or moth. The four stages form what experts call a complete metamorphosis.

. . . a beautiful moth like this!

THE LIFE CYCLE OF A MOURNING CLOAK BUTTERFLY

eggs   *chrysalis*

larva (on elm tree leaf)

adult butterfly

The larval stage is known by a very common name—caterpillar. The pupal stage is the dormant or resting stage in which these as yet unborn butterflies and moths pass the winter. Normally after hibernating outdoors over the winter months, the chrysalids open up, the cocoons split open, and out come bedraggled creatures with the six legs of the true insects. But attached to their backs is a tightly folded, crumpled, and dampened pair of wings. The insect crawls out on twig, flower, or leaf, where the sun can reach it. As he begins pumping fluid into the veins of his wings, these gradually unfold. Moving them slowly up and down, the butterfly or moth soon dries its wings and is ready to fly off. Now, of course, is the time to release your specimen.

BOOK LIST

Here is a book list that will help you explore further the world of nature and nature activities:

GENERAL BOOKS:

Field Book of Nature Activities, William Hillcourt; G. P. Putnam's Sons, N. Y.; 1950

The Book of Nature Hobbies, Ted Pettit; Didier Publishing Co., N. Y.; 1947

Hammond's Guide to Nature Hobbies, Dr. E. L. Jordan; C. S. Hammond & Co., N. Y.; 1953

The Amateur Naturalist's Handbook, Vinson Brown; Little, Brown & Co., Boston; 1948

The Book of Wild Pets, Clifford B. Moore; Charles T. Branford Co., Boston; 1954

Books that will give you more information on the various activities described in this book:

FEATHERS ARE FABULOUS:

A Field Guide to the Birds, Roger Tory Peterson; Houghton Mifflin Co., Boston; 1947

Birds: A Guide to the Most Familiar American Birds, H. S. Zim and I. N. Gabrielson; Simon & Schuster, N. Y.; 1949

CASTING ANIMAL TRACKS:

Tracks and Trailcraft, Ellsworth Jaeger; Macmillan Co., N. Y.; 1948

Animal Tracks, George F. Mason; William Morrow & Co., N. Y.; 1943

HOW TO BE A ROCK HOUND:

Rocks and Minerals, H. S. Zim and P. R. Shaffer; Simon & Schuster, N. Y.; 1957

Minerals—Their Identification, Uses, and How To Collect Them, H. S. Zim and Elizabeth K. Cooper; Harcourt, Brace & Co., N. Y.; 1943

A Field Guide to Rocks and Minerals, Frederick H. Pough; Houghton Mifflin Co., Boston; 1953

SPIDER WEBS ARE AMAZING:

The Spider's Web, Theodore H. Savory; Frederick Warne & Co., Ltd., London and N. Y.; 1952

American Spiders, W. J. Gertsch; D. Van Nostrand Co., Inc., N. Y.; 1949

WINDOW GARDENS FROM KITCHEN CUTTINGS:

Picture Primer of Indoor Gardening, Margaret O. Goldsmith; Houghton Mifflin Co., Boston; 1946

Garden Indoors, Bertha Morris Parker; Row, Peterson & Co., White Plains, N. Y., and Evanston, Ill.; 1953

EXPLORING A STREAM:

Wild Folk at the Pond, Carroll Lane Fenton; The John Day Company, N. Y.; 1948

Beginner's Guide to Fresh Water Life, Leon A. Hausman; G. P. Putnam's Sons, N. Y.; 1949

MAKING LEAF PRINTS AND LEAF SKELETONS:

Learn the Trees from Leaf Prints, David S. Marx; Botanic Publishing Co., Cincinnati, Ohio; 1938

LEARN WHERE ANIMALS LIVE:

Animal Homes, George F. Mason; William Morrow & Co., N. Y.; 1947

Some Animals and Their Homes, Mary G. Phillips and Julia M. Wright; D. C. Heath & Co., N. Y.; 1936

EGGSHELL GARDENS:

Garden in Your Window, Jean Hersey; Prentice-Hall, Inc., N. Y.; 1949

Play With Plants, Millicent E. Selsam; William Morrow & Co., N. Y.; 1949

MAKE SEEDS SPROUT:

The First Book of Plants, Alice Dickinson; Franklin Watts, Inc., N. Y.; 1953

Plants in the City, Herman and Nina Schneider; The John Day Company, N. Y.; 1951

COLLECTING BUTTERFLIES:

A Field Guide to the Butterflies, Alexander B. Klots; Houghton Mifflin Co., Boston; 1951

The Junior Book of Insects, Edwin Way Teale: E. P. Dutton & Co., N. Y.; 1953

MAKING A DESERT GARDEN INDOORS:

Exotic Plants, Alfred Byrd Graf; Julius Roehrs Co., Rutherford, N. J.; 1953

COLLECTING WOOD IS FUN:

Knowing Your Trees, G. H. Collingwood and Warren D. Brush; The American Forestry Association, Washington, D. C.; 1947

Trees, H. S. Zim and A. Martin; Simon & Schuster, N. Y.; Revised Edition, 1956

FRIENDLY FELLOWS IN YOUR GARDEN:

How To Attract The Birds, Robert S. Lemmon; The American Garden Guild, Inc., and Doubleday & Co., Garden City, N. Y.; 1947

Toads and Frogs, Bertha Morris Parker; Row, Peterson & Co., White Plains, N. Y., and Evanston, Ill.; 1942

STARGAZING:

Stars, H. S. Zim and R. H. Baker; Simon & Schuster, N. Y.; Revised Edition, 1956

The Golden Book of Astronomy, Rose Wyler and Gerald Ames; Simon & Schuster, N. Y.; 1955

The Sky Observer's Guide, Mayall, Mayall, and Wyckoff; Golden Press, N. Y.; 1959

PLAY SANTA TO YOUR BIRD FRIENDS:

Handbook of Attracting Birds, Thomas P. McElroy, Jr.; Alfred P. Knopf, N. Y.; 1951

Song Birds in Your Garden, John K. Terres; Thomas Y. Crowell Co., N. Y.; 1953

WHERE DO ANIMALS GO IN WINTER?:

Field Book of Animals in Winter, Ann Haven Morgan; G. P. Putnam's Sons, N. Y.; 1939

Natural Science Through the Seasons, J. A. Partridge; The Macmillan Company of Canada, Toronto; 1955

TROPICAL FISH:

Tropical Fishes as Pets, C. W. Coates; Liveright Publishing Co., N. Y.; Revised Edition, 1950

True Book of Tropical Fishes, Ray Broekel; Children's Press, Chicago; 1956

BUILD AND FILL AN INSECT ZOO:

Field Book of Insects, Frank E. Lutz; G. P. Putnam's Sons, N. Y.; Revised Edition, 1948

Insects, H. S. Zim and C. Cottam; Simon & Schuster, N. Y.; Revised Edition, 1956

BUTTERFLIES AND MOTHS:

Collecting Cocoons, Lois J. Hussey and Catherine Pessino; Thomas Y. Crowell Co., N. Y.; 1953

The Insect Guide, Ralph B. Swain; Doubleday & Co., Inc., Garden City, N. Y.; 1948